Matryoshka Houses

Matryoshka Houses

Poems by

Lynn Pattison

Cover Design by Shay Culligan
Cover art by Mindi Bagnall

ISBN: 978-1-952326-25-7

Kelsay Books
502 South 1040 East, A-119
American Fork, Utah, 84003

In memory of my parents, Rodney and Dorothy Hutchinson,
and my sister, Karen Lawrence

Acknowledgments

I am grateful to the editors of the following journals and reviews in which these poems first appeared (some in slightly different form):

Adanna Literary Journal: "Soup," "Starve"

Atlanta Review: "Rustbeltasana"

Mom Egg Review: "Still, it all seemed about the same until we buried you"

The 3288 Review: "Matryoshka houses," "Elusive"

Tinderbox Poetry Journal: "Cleaning the birdhouse"

In Transitions: An Anthology of Women's Poetry (published with the chapbook "*Skin Gin*," QuillsEdge Press),: "Elusive"

I am grateful to the artists and writers who participated in Home: *An Artists and Writers Project* (2014-2015), whose creative interpretations and explorations lent inspiration to some of these poems, and to the members of my poetry group, Poetry Dawgs, who give of themselves so generously. Thank you to Jim Kates and the Association of Writers & Writing Programs for support and encouragement.

Contents

My pyramid

Each new home settled atop the last
thick overlaying   drawing its nature
          from the course beneath.

The house of my childhood
nooks and arches   curving stairs
          then house of right angles

the home where I raised babies
threadbare   fading
          but friendly.

The place of blended family.
The cabin   white pine and the river
broad base
ascending layers

each shaded and colored
by the last—just as we paint
          each new love or betrayal

with brushes from the old paintbox—
until the house is home
          split geode   leaf skeleton

perfect as when we found it
spoons from the farmhouse that burned
          hosta from the old yard

ghosts of grief and joy weave
between potted plants that purified the air
     in one house   tempted

the dog in the next   not a perfect
polyhedron   but standing   steadfast
     no matter the weather

Elusive

Kaleidoscope rooflines—sloped, hipped,
   gabled. Sunroom overlaid with driveway, porch,

as if someone's playing with double exposures,
   jamming slides into the projector all at once. The story

of home can't be unearthed by orderly excavation,
   studied one stratum at a time—even if you run string

in quadrants, label religiously. Jumble
of wax pilgrims and jewelry boxes with dancers

on the lids, framed diplomas and watering cans,
   sump pumps and inner tubes. Here, a bedroom lit

with northern light, another washed warm
   from the south. Part of the story is what the kids

carried off to apartments, what sold
   before the move to Florida. Time parses old input

through translucent scrims, and memory
   does a kind of collapsing—filing system as collage,

as Drummond Island puddingstone: spotty cluster
   of red jasper, chert and quartz. Keep an open mind.

If you insist on orderly narrative, one slide
   after the other, you won't get the whole effect.

Still, it all seemed about the same until we buried you

Back in Ypsilanti the city stretches right out to meet me
at I-94: car wash, Tim Horton's, 7-11.

Center city's grown dismal: blank storefronts,buildings missing.
Like your uncle's drugstore, lost to fire,

that gap-toothed look, middle of the old brick block.
The river no longer runs past Frog Island

in oranges or blues depending on the color craft paper
they're making at the mill.

The old high school's turned senior housing, now,
and the ladder company's boarded up.

A renaissance down at the depot: antiques and restaurants,
florists and farmers' market. The college

has expanded into the woods where we fell in creeks,
climbed trees. Mornings, girls and boys

don't walk to school up two hills, over a bridge
and on past the fire station, Stark's Funeral Home.

The public library's moved from the stone manse
where I mended books Saturdays

in a dusty back room, up to my elbows in glue and strips
of stiff binding cloth. Standing by your headstone,

I see the Catholic cemetery has sprawled and filled,
and across the road fresh Protestant graves

scatter like wildflowers over new grass. On Maple Street
a family's borrowing our photos, restoring our old house.

Toward midnight

A thin doe on the farthest green
breaks snow crust to nibble grass
that Sam, the grounds man,
has, he'd say, *busted my ass*

all winter to protect. He'll curse
the damage her need has left
thinking what her hunger's cost,
then soften, spotting tracks of fawns.

And in her night-blue kitchen Annette,
both Labs pressing against her knees,
listens to her mom's regrets
and thinks she'll manage to free

her from at least one anxiety,
promising, yes, she'll drive over
in the morning with coffee;
yes, the grandchildren love her ...

On I-94 a load of eggs
jackknifes on ice. It takes Ed Gault
and his men three hours to scrape
things down, spread sand and salt

enough to reopen the stretch.
They look into the dark sky, ease
their trucks off the shoulder's edge,
and turn. Back in town, Ed leaves

a block's worth of ice and snow
accidentally on the driveway
apron of the damn fool coach
who cut Ed Junior from varsity.

Passing later, he'll feel sad,
seeing the guy shoveling, sweating,
yelling at his own boy to put his *back
into it,* in his too-small woolen hat.

Two blocks down, Wanda Blake's son
shows up after seven months to rake
roof snow and shovel the drive. He's gone
by sun up, heading for the lake,

his fish shanty. He stops at the grade
of Burlington Northern track
where two engines push a plow blade
tall as a water tower through packed

snow and ice. Wide white wings
bloom from either side as if some
commanding angel sweeps across
the prairie in moonlight delirium.

Cleaning the birdhouse

So many things
A mother can't explain

how a toad
gets down a wire

into a birdhouse,
why it wants

to be there   and
            about the one

pale blue egg
that falls too

onto the dry
August grass.

Rustbeltasana

Stand tall, feet rooted in the soil
of the pioneers. Legs straight,

body aligned, head floating
like a corn tassel above stalks.

With shoulders back and eyes
forward, pull your pockets inside out.

Avoid gazing out windows with views
of abandoned factories, vacant houses.

Bend over, hands on floor. Lower self
to knees. Hold. Rise if you can.

Quandaries: depot town

Why the river runs violet.
We smell sweat burning on the surface of coal.
The stones in the roadbed don't rattle down
                the grade and disappear.
What dangerous language is written on boxcars?
I know only one side of Frog Island.

Even here the odor of pressing cloth and starch
                Tuesday's baskets of ironing.
An infinite regress of my reflection   and the train
that never entirely vanishes at the horizon.

Soup

shank of hard knocks
        cheesecloth bundle of thorns
and thimbleberry cane   all depend on the simmer
        and how you brave the steam

experiment: roe   spelt   pig's blood
        coconut milk & puffballs
don't be afraid of salt   let onion tears fall
        into the broth

a twist of tobacco   smudge of rennet
        pinch of fungus from cistern wall
yesterday's coffee
        tomorrow's wine

oak gall   a page from the divorce decree
        paper always starts as soup
Swiss chard and mustard leaves
        for envy   vinegar for fear

reduce past reason   fortify
        with powdered antler
add the tongue from your old leather boot
        angst makes it meaty

no one likes thin soup
        steep & stir
you never saw what your mother
        added mid-afternoon

Starve

a fever, and those clouds that fatten on the horizon
threaten to rain again on the bowed and beaten blossoms
by the walk, the voice under your third rib that whispers *flat*

as you begin your song & *wrong* as you raise bow to strings.
Don't starve the artist in his unheated rooms any longer.
He paints his hunger in oils he's forced to dilute,

on the only paper he can find, a remarkable effect
that leaves his cousins wealthy after he's gone. Deny
the river one more mouthful of collapsing bluff, wildfires

in western canyons one more gulp of hilltop timber. Withhold
water from pots of ivy you bring inside for overwintering—
a signal they'll need to harden down.

They say what grows in us is the part we feed.
You can starve a house to sticks, but it takes a while.
Oh to deprive cancers that chew through bodies of too many

friends, growing like a child's crystal garden. In the corner
a spider finds no prey where I swept away flies, and in the grate
flames thin when I shut the glass doors.

Stars blink, faint behind a veil of snow,
rumbling hunger for the human gaze, the heat
that rises from where we watch in summer. What if

somehow we starved the moon, and it wasted to nothing,
no red eclipse, no tidal bore, always the unlit path
at midnight? What if we could see

the hidden fevers we feed each day, that consume
our light and repay us with darkness, the twisted limbs
that slow us down. The things we need to tie off until they wither.

The thing behind, and the thing behind that

I can't see why grief brought me here to this kitchen
    too small for baking, to rolling pin and breadboard.

These are illogical days; nothing seems to follow
    reasonably another. I've given up on cause & effect.

Guilt's like that, the more you dig for the root,
    the more suckers you find branching sideways,

curling into the mud. Today I'm baking bread—
    stirring, kneading, punching down. It's been thirty years.

Warm like earth in spring, this elastic dough I turn
    and braid and mark, brought alive by a sprinkle of yeast

on warm water. Rocking rhythm between the heels
    of my hands and the give of gluten. Wind howls

a word I've never heard, repeating—
    I know better than to think I can translate.

After rain, November

Fog over the Pigeon River. Light
whispers between cedar and pine.
Up on the bluff, it's a cloudy day, but I climb
down the bank into fog. In the haze
above rapids, water mumbles

to overwintering birds and I breathe
in the last of November's mild days.
Ferns brown and bend, yet here
is a wave of new growth needles
on spruce and cedar. This is an understory world,

wet leaves underfoot. A few
corn cobs dragged from the squirrel feeder.
Across the river, white-barked birches
among the evergreens,
slight limbs longing skyward.

The text for the day is *reach*
in this chapel—the best at yearning
toward the sun will see the decade out.
November rains bless these woods.
One more drink before dry cold comes.

Not until the song

The north corner holds after fire, straining to pull the rest
        back into shape. Water creeps into bedrooms,
then clear through to cellar. Shutters tear away in wind that slams
        and opens and slams the front door until it blows,

end over end, into the drive. Passersby peer in at soot stain
        and a broken stove. Note the dried flypaper coils.
Upstairs a sink suspended in space above the kitchen. This place
        is dead to them. But if mice who once skittered

across the doorsill still venture through, still nibble
        gleaned corn in familiar corners, if my father
remembers his father setting logs at dawn, his mother humming
        as she works the churn or winds yarn around

her son's hands, life remains. The house echoes
        its old language—words that murmured the halls,
phrases that scaled the staircase. Calls that reached to the pasture
        if they had to. *Here,* the house sings, *here I am.*

The dog, if I had one. Maybe my pillow.

Making my way back to the hotel in Cancun,
   weak after sickness on water, all I want is my bed.
      I want to get *home,* I say, the concept suddenly reduced

to a room with an ocean view, the particular bed
   I've occupied for a few days, the concierge who will tut-tut
      and call the elevator. I would have said it took longer to set

 the feel of home. Childhood in the same house,
   friends at school and down the block or decades raising a family
      in one spot. Place of friendships, work, play, and familiar faces.

Traditions and routine. But a grandmother
   moving into elder care must choose a spatter of belongings
      to mean she's home. The homeless carry

their world in plastic bags—home any place they lay
   their bedroll. In my case, a room, suitcase and bed
      became the home I was desperate for. My normal home

irrelevant. Pioneers crossed the wilderness
   in wagons, home reduced to sticks and canvas,
      the family bed surrounded by flour barrels, shovels.

Anne, house lost to fire, transplanted
   her mother's catmint and spiderwort to her new home.
      If I were on the run, a refugee, what would I carry? Water

in a plastic jug? Bread knife? Straw hat?
   Not my souvenir figure of Queen Elizabeth waving
      from the sill on sunny days. Not the breadbox

or books. A handful of photos,
   of course. Birth certificate. My mother's
      silver chain, door key on it for when I make it back.

He browses college catalogs in the
Los Angeles Library

Filtered light, the atmosphere a seep of gray.
A photo distinct from all others on the page—
the look of home, here between the lakes.

My son in California calls to say
he knew at once the Kalamazoo landscape:
its filtered light, the atmosphere a seep of gray.

Not the street or college buildings per se,
but the way clouds mist brick in a sepia haze.
The familiar look of home, here between the lakes.

A climate he can read as easily as his name
from one snapshot in a catalog. Can't mistake
that dim light and atmosphere of weepy gray

in which he walked to school on February days.
Far off in a southern wash of sun, he nearly tastes
the weather of his childhood home between the lakes.

Though LA's where he'll stay, he says,
suddenly, deeply, he misses this place
of filtered light. The atmosphere and seep of gray,
the look of home. Here between the lakes.

Carnival life

My home is an old Ferris wheel,
rising high in a prairie sky, where I travel steadily
but never go anywhere. Sailing backward over the midway

brings new perspectives. Returning
and returning, changes after each swoop: calliope tune,
faces in the ticket line. No control over who boards—pickpocket

or priest. The smells of sweat and frying oil
permeate the seats, and my fingerprints are thick
along the crash bar. When the motor threatens to seize up,

the wheel vibrates with tension. I get queasy.
The price of tickets balloons, the budget's strained.
When the press shows up, I hope it's for Miss Michigan,

not another Tilt-A-Whirl disaster.
I dream of unbolting my car at the top, flying free
above barkers, coin-toss games and the Tunnel of Love

into green and golden fields.
Some say you can't go back, though Lula says
you really can't leave and the fortune teller's never wrong.

At Last

A woodchuck waddles from the thicket
to lunch on young shoots. The marsh rings
with cries of peepers—Easter creatures, with crosses
on their tiny backs. I want to wind the trunks

of saplings in blue ribbon, hang flags over
the door. Soon we'll clean feeders and brew syrup
for the hummingbirds waiting for bee balm and bleeding
heart. A clutch of turkeys cuts

across the path, males fanning full displays.
Under a mat of leaves, tulips nudge up, appraise
the light. I tie prayer scrolls in the sweetgum,
cut woody vines from trees. Soon

a haze of green in the treetops and soil
softening. Time for wind chimes of hollow bones,
bottles that whistle. Tomorrow, mayapples
unfurling, lilies of the valley rising. Ovenbirds.

Matryoshka houses

Cunning construct of time and light. Close this one
into that, see how they fit inside each other. Fit me.

One me or another. The cedar home in the woods halves open,
revealing a green, high-peaked house (place of telescoping hours).

What was it that lived there with us, ghosting shadows
in the corner of my eye? Inside: the low, gray bungalow,

rooms flooded pink with sun through the crab apple.
Deepest in, most tightly held: red brick, rounded door,

house of attics and cubbies, platter-sized records
played on the Victrola, a pipe stand. Music rises from them all:

big band, folk, rock & roll (all of it a wild-looping canon—
pitch and speed staggered—crabbing memories, remixing).

Fragments of melody pushing and stacking the years.
Brass doorknobs, root cellar damp, sisters wrapping apples

to store in barrels, singing *Panis Angelicus* off-key.
In one house, kids arrive, a husband leaves. A basement laundry

where we huddled as midnight sirens wailed,
where the dog whimpered and peed every Fourth of July.

My mother's song hums below each roof, flows
between walls—sewing the years. Snow drifts at one door

while leaves fall around the next. Heat. Lightning. Voices echo
as if down long halls. When the fog moves in, I take them all apart.

About the Author

Lynn Pattison lives with her husband, Richard, in Southwest Michigan. Her poems have appeared in *The Notre Dame Review, Rhino, Pinyon,* and *Smartish Pace,* among others, and been anthologized in several publications. She is the author of three poetry collections: *tesla's daughter* (March St. Press), *Walking Back the Cat* (Bright Hill Press), and *Light That Sounds Like Breaking* (Mayapple Press). Pattison's work has been nominated for Pushcart recognition and inclusion in *Best Small Fictions.* She has been supported in her writing by an Irving S. Gilmore artist's grant, The Ragdale Foundation, and the AWP Writer to Writer Program.

✍